REAL ESTATE CROWDFUNDING AND SHORT-TERM RENTAL ARBITRAG

Unlocking Wealth with Proven Strategies for Successful Investment

Gleen William

Table of Contents

INTRODUCTION: NAVIGATING THE TERRAIN OF REAL ESTATE CROWDFUNDING AND SHORT-TERM RENTAL ARBITRAGE

Real estate investment has evolved significantly in recent years, with innovative approaches offering opportunities for both passive and active income streams. Two such strategies, Real Estate Crowdfunding and Short-Term Rental Arbitrage, have gained prominence in the investment landscape. Understanding these approaches and their potential synergies is crucial for those seeking to capitalize on the dynamic real estate market.

Overview of Real Estate Crowdfunding:

Real Estate Crowdfunding represents a paradigm shift in how individuals can participate in real estate ventures without the traditional barriers to entry. This method involves pooling funds from a large number of investors to finance a real estate project. Unlike conventional real estate investment, crowdfunding allows individuals to invest with smaller amounts of capital, providing a more inclusive avenue for wealth creation.

The key advantages of Real Estate Crowdfunding include diversification of investments across various projects, reduced financial risk through shared responsibility, and access to a broader range of real estate opportunities. Investors can choose from different types of crowdfunding models, such as equity-based or debt-based, depending on their risk tolerance and investment goals.

Understanding Short-Term Rental Arbitrage:

Short-Term Rental Arbitrage is a hands-on strategy that involves leasing a property on a long-term basis and renting it out on short-term platforms like Airbnb or VRBO for higher nightly rates. This approach requires careful management of bookings, property maintenance, and a keen understanding of the local rental market.

The appeal of Short-Term Rental Arbitrage lies in its potential for higher returns compared to traditional long-term rentals.

By leveraging the sharing economy and catering to the growing demand for short-term stays, investors can capitalize on premium pricing, especially in tourist-heavy or business-centric locations.

The Synergy Between Crowdfunding and Arbitrage:

The intersection of Real Estate Crowdfunding and Short-Term Rental Arbitrage presents a unique opportunity for investors to diversify their portfolios and create a balanced approach to real estate investment. While crowdfunding offers a passive and diversified income stream, arbitrage adds an active, income-generating component to the strategy.

Investors can benefit from the stability and potential appreciation offered by crowdfunding projects, while simultaneously tapping into the immediate cash flow provided by short-term rental arbitrage. This combination allows for a more dynamic and resilient investment strategy, mitigating risks associated with market fluctuations and economic uncertainties.

Understanding these two approaches individually is essential, but recognizing the synergies between them can elevate your investment strategy to new heights. As we delve deeper into the intricacies of Real Estate Crowdfunding and Short-Term Rental Arbitrage, we'll explore how to integrate these strategies seamlessly and create a holistic investment plan that maximizes returns while managing risks effectively. Whether you're a seasoned investor or a newcomer to the real estate scene, the journey through these strategies promises valuable insights and actionable steps towards financial success in the ever-evolving world of real estate investment.

Reader Engagement Section: Reflect and Apply

Now that you've delved into the world of Real Estate Crowdfunding, take a moment to reflect on how this model aligns with your investment goals. Consider the following questions:

I. What specific aspects of crowdfunding appeal to you, and how do they align with your investment strategy?

II. Are there particular types of real estate projects within crowdfunding that resonate with your interests or risk tolerance?

III. How might you adapt the principles discussed in this chapter to your unique financial situation and goals?

REAL ESTATE CROWDFUNDING: NAVIGATING THE LANDSCAPE OF COLLECTIVE INVESTMENT

The Concept of Crowdfunding in Real Estate:

Real Estate Crowdfunding transforms the traditional landscape of property investment by democratizing access to real estate projects. At its core, crowdfunding is about harnessing the collective financial power of numerous individuals to fund a real estate venture. This method allows investors to contribute relatively small amounts of capital, breaking down the financial barriers that often accompany real estate investment.

Within the realm of Real Estate Crowdfunding, there are two primary models: equity-based and debt-based crowdfunding. In equity-based crowdfunding, investors become partial owners of the property, sharing in its potential appreciation and rental income.

On the other hand, debt-based crowdfunding involves investors providing loans to real estate developers in exchange for fixed interest payments. Understanding these models is crucial as they define the nature of the investment and the returns investors can expect.

Benefits and Risks of Real Estate Crowdfunding:

Real Estate Crowdfunding presents several compelling benefits for investors seeking exposure to the real estate market without the burden of significant capital outlay. Diversification is a key advantage; investors can spread their capital across multiple projects, reducing the risk associated with a single investment. Additionally, crowdfunding provides access to a variety of real estate opportunities, from residential developments to commercial properties, allowing investors to tailor their portfolios to match their preferences and risk tolerance.

The potential for passive income is another significant advantage.

Unlike traditional real estate ownership, where active involvement is often required, Real Estate Crowdfunding allows investors to enjoy returns without the day-to-day responsibilities of property management. This passive income stream makes it an attractive option for those seeking hands-off real estate investments.

However, like any investment, Real Estate Crowdfunding comes with its share of risks. Market fluctuations, project delays, or unexpected costs can impact returns. It's crucial for investors to conduct thorough due diligence on crowdfunding platforms and individual projects, understanding the associated risks before committing capital. Additionally, the relatively illiquid nature of real estate investments means that funds may be tied up for an extended period, making it important for investors to align their investment horizon with their financial goals.

Popular Real Estate Crowdfunding Platforms:

The success of a Real Estate Crowdfunding investment often hinges on the choice of the crowdfunding platform.

Several platforms have emerged, each with its unique features, project selection, and fee structures. Some well-established platforms include Fundrise, Realty Mogul, and Crowd Street.

Fundrise, for instance, is known for its easy-to-use platform and diversified investment options. Investors can choose from various portfolios, each tailored to different risk profiles and investment goals. Realty Mogul specializes in both debt and equity investments, offering a range of projects from apartment complexes to commercial properties. Crowd Street, on the other hand, focuses on commercial real estate, connecting investors with institutional-quality deals.

How to Get Started with Real Estate Crowdfunding:

Getting started with Real Estate Crowdfunding involves a strategic approach that aligns with individual financial goals and risk tolerance. The following steps can guide investors through the process:

Educate Yourself: Before diving in, educate yourself about the fundamentals of real estate crowdfunding, understand the different models, and familiarize yourself with the risks and rewards.

Establish Investment Objectives: Clearly state your objectives for investing. Are you looking for long-term appreciation, regular income, or a combination of both? Knowing your goals will help you make the right investment decisions.

Select a Reputable Platform: Research and select a reputable crowdfunding platform that aligns with your investment goals. Consider factors such as the platform's track record, project selection, and fee structure.

Diversify Your Investments: Spread your investments across multiple projects or portfolios to mitigate risk. Diversification is a key strategy in building a resilient real estate investment portfolio.

Conduct Due Diligence: Thoroughly research and evaluate potential projects before committing capital. Review project details, financial projections, and the track record of the development team.

Real Estate Crowdfunding offers a gateway for individuals to participate in real estate projects, providing both financial accessibility and diversification. By understanding the concept, benefits, and risks, and by adopting a careful, informed approach, investors can navigate the world of Real Estate Crowdfunding with confidence.

In the subsequent sections, we will delve into the intricacies of Short-Term Rental Arbitrage, exploring its potential and how it can complement Real Estate Crowdfunding in a comprehensive investment strategy.

Reader Engagement Section: Apply Your Knowledge

As you explore the intricacies of Short-Term Rental Arbitrage, it's time to consider how these strategies can be applied to your real estate endeavors. Take a moment to:

I. Identify potential locations in your area that could be suitable for short-term rentals. What factors make these locations attractive?

II. Develop a basic plan for negotiating a long-term lease that aligns with arbitrage principles. What terms and conditions would you prioritize?

III. Consider how you might optimize the presentation and amenities of a short-term rental property to enhance guest satisfaction and attract positive reviews.

SHORT-TERM RENTAL ARBITRAGE: UNLOCKING INCOME THROUGH DYNAMIC LEASING STRATEGIES

Exploring the Basics of Short-Term Rental Arbitrage:

Short-Term Rental Arbitrage is a dynamic strategy that taps into the sharing economy to generate income from property leasing. At its core, this approach involves leasing a property on a long-term basis and subsequently renting it out on short-term platforms such as Airbnb, VRBO, or Booking.com. The key to success lies in securing the property at a favorable long-term lease rate and then strategically pricing short-term rentals to capitalize on the demand for temporary accommodations.

One of the primary attractions of Short-Term Rental Arbitrage is its potential for higher returns compared to traditional long-term rentals.

By catering to the growing trend of travelers seeking unique and personalized accommodation experiences, investors can command premium rates for short stays, especially in desirable locations.

Pros and Cons of Short-Term Rental Investments:

Short-Term Rental Arbitrage offers a range of advantages that contribute to its popularity among investors seeking active income streams:

Higher Rental Income: The ability to charge higher nightly rates for short stays often results in greater overall rental income compared to traditional long-term leases.

Flexibility and Control: Short-Term Rental hosts have more flexibility in managing their properties. They can block dates for personal use, make adjustments to pricing, and optimize occupancy based on market trends.

Adaptability to Market Conditions: Short-Term Rental hosts can quickly adapt to changing market conditions.

They can adjust pricing strategies based on seasonal demand, local events, or other factors impacting the rental market.

However, like any investment strategy, Short-Term Rental Arbitrage comes with its set of challenges and considerations:

Operational Demands: Managing short-term rentals requires a hands-on approach. Tasks include guest communication, property maintenance, and adhering to local regulations, demanding a certain level of operational commitment.

Market Sensitivity: The short-term rental market can be sensitive to external factors such as economic downturns, travel restrictions, or shifts in consumer preferences. Hosts must stay attuned to market dynamics to optimize their strategies.

Key Considerations Before Engaging in Arbitrage:

Before embarking on a Short-Term Rental Arbitrage venture, it's crucial to consider several key factors to maximize success:

Location Selection: Choose a location with high demand for short-term rentals. Proximity to tourist attractions, business centers, or popular events can significantly impact the property's rental potential.

Lease Negotiation Skills: Successful arbitrage hinges on securing favorable long-term lease terms. Develop negotiation skills to secure reasonable rent rates that allow for profitable short-term rentals.

Understanding Regulations: Familiarize yourself with local regulations and zoning laws related to short-term rentals. Compliance is essential to avoid legal issues that could jeopardize the profitability of the venture.

Property Presentation: Invest in the presentation of your property. Quality furnishings, cleanliness, and thoughtful amenities contribute to positive guest experiences, leading to favorable reviews and repeat bookings.

Optimizing Property Selection for Short-Term Rentals:

The success of Short-Term Rental Arbitrage also depends on selecting properties that align with the preferences of short-term renters. When selecting a property, take into account the following:

Size and Layout: Opt for properties that cater to the target market. Larger units may attract families, while smaller, centrally located spaces may appeal to solo travelers or couples.

Amenities: Provide amenities that enhance the guest experience. This could include fully equipped kitchens, high-speed internet, and convenient check-in processes.

Competitive Pricing: Research the local market to determine competitive pricing. Setting reasonable rates while offering value ensures a steady stream of bookings.

Synergies Between Crowdfunding and Short-Term Rental Models:

While Real Estate Crowdfunding and Short-Term Rental Arbitrage operate as distinct strategies, there are synergies that investors can leverage for a holistic approach to real estate investment. Combining the stability and potential appreciation of crowdfunding with the immediate income-generating capability of arbitrage creates a balanced and diversified investment strategy.

Investors can allocate funds to crowdfunding projects for long-term growth and stability, while simultaneously engaging in short-term rental arbitrage to generate ongoing income. This dual approach allows for resilience against market fluctuations, economic uncertainties, and provides a dynamic investment portfolio that adapts to evolving market conditions.

As we navigate the landscape of Short-Term Rental Arbitrage, it becomes evident that strategic property selection, operational efficiency, and a keen understanding of market dynamics are paramount to success.

In the subsequent sections, we will explore the integration of these two strategies, offering actionable insights for investors seeking to maximize returns through a comprehensive real estate investment plan.

Reader Engagement Section: Strategic Planning

As you explore the dynamic world of Short-Term Rental Arbitrage, it's time to strategically plan your entry into this market. Reflect on the following:

I. Select a potential location for your arbitrage venture. What factors make this location promising for short-term rentals?

II. Develop a negotiation strategy for securing favorable long-term lease terms.

III. How can you maximize your profit margins while ensuring a win-win for all parties involved?

IV. Consider the key elements that will make your short-term rental property stand out. How can you create a unique and memorable experience for guests?

COMBINING STRATEGIES: REAL ESTATE CROWDFUNDING AND SHORT-TERM RENTAL ARBITRAGE

Synergies between Crowdfunding and Short-Term Rental Models:

The fusion of Real Estate Crowdfunding and Short-Term Rental Arbitrage creates a potent investment strategy that capitalizes on the strengths of both approaches. While Real Estate Crowdfunding offers stability, long-term growth potential, and diversification, Short-Term Rental Arbitrage introduces the element of immediate, active income generation. Understanding the synergies between these models is essential for investors aiming to build a resilient and dynamic real estate portfolio.

One of the primary advantages of combining these strategies lies in risk mitigation. Real Estate Crowdfunding, by nature, provides a diversified investment portfolio across various projects, property types, and geographic locations.

This diversification helps to spread risk and reduce exposure to the potential downsides of a single investment. On the other hand, Short-Term Rental Arbitrage introduces an active income stream, adding a layer of financial resilience that can offset any fluctuations in the crowdfunding portfolio.

Diversifying Investments in Real Estate:

Diversification is a fundamental principle in investment strategy, and the combination of Crowdfunding and Arbitrage allows for diversification both within and outside the real estate market. Within real estate, Crowdfunding platforms often offer a range of project types, including residential, commercial, and development projects. Investors can diversify their crowdfunding portfolio by strategically selecting projects with varying risk profiles and potential returns.

Simultaneously, Short-Term Rental Arbitrage enables investors to diversify their income streams by engaging in different types of rental properties.

For instance, a well-balanced portfolio might include short-term rentals in tourist-heavy areas, corporate rentals in business districts, and even seasonal rentals in recreational destinations.

This diversity in rental strategies not only enhances income potential but also provides resilience in the face of changing market conditions.

Managing Risks and Maximizing Returns:

Successful investment is about balancing risks and returns. The combination of Real Estate Crowdfunding and Short-Term Rental Arbitrage allows investors to manage risks effectively while optimizing returns through a thoughtful, integrated approach.

Risk Management in Crowdfunding: Crowdfunding platforms typically conduct thorough due diligence on projects, providing investors with insights into the potential risks and returns. Investors can further mitigate risks by diversifying across different projects, geographic regions, and property types. Regular monitoring and staying informed about market trends contribute to effective risk management.

Risk Mitigation in Arbitrage: Short-Term Rental Arbitrage carries operational risks, such as property management challenges, regulatory changes, or unexpected market shifts.

Investors can mitigate these risks by staying informed about local regulations, maintaining excellent property management practices, and adapting rental strategies based on market conditions.

Enhancing Returns through Synergy: The synergy between Crowdfunding and Arbitrage allows investors to enhance returns through complementary strategies. The stable, long-term growth potential of crowdfunding aligns well with the more immediate income-generating nature of arbitrage. Returns from successful crowdfunding projects can be reinvested into additional arbitrage opportunities, creating a cycle of growth and income generation.

Implementation Strategies:

Implementing a combined strategy involves a strategic allocation of resources and a clear plan for execution. Consider the following steps:

Portfolio Allocation: Determine the percentage of your real estate investment portfolio allocated to crowdfunding and arbitrage. This allocation should align with your financial goals, risk tolerance, and investment horizon.

Research and Due Diligence: Conduct thorough research on crowdfunding platforms and potential projects. Similarly, analyze the local market dynamics, property values, and rental demand for short-term arbitrage opportunities. Due diligence is critical to informed decision-making.

Timing and Coordination: Consider the timing of your investments and arbitrage activities. Coordination between the two strategies can optimize cash flow and ensure that returns from one aspect of the portfolio can support investments or operational needs in the other.

Continuous Monitoring: Regularly monitor the performance of both crowdfunding projects and short-term rentals. Evaluate the success of your strategies, adapt to changing market conditions, and make informed adjustments to your portfolio as needed.

By carefully integrating Real Estate Crowdfunding and Short-Term Rental Arbitrage, investors can create a comprehensive and resilient real estate investment plan.

The synergy between these strategies not only enhances financial outcomes but also provides a flexible approach that can adapt to the ever-evolving dynamics of the real estate market. As we move forward, case studies will illustrate successful implementations of this combined approach, offering practical insights and inspiration for investors seeking to optimize their real estate portfolios.

Reader Engagement Section: Integrating Your Plan

Now that you understand the synergies between Crowdfunding and Arbitrage, it's time to integrate these strategies into your own investment plan. Reflect on the following:

I. Determine the percentage of your portfolio allocated to crowdfunding and arbitrage. How can you strike a balance that aligns with your financial goals and risk tolerance?

II. Research potential crowdfunding projects while simultaneously exploring short-term rental opportunities. How can you ensure a seamless integration of both strategies?

III. Consider how returns from crowdfunding projects can strategically support your short-term rental ventures. How will you reinvest returns for maximum impact?

30-DAY ACTION PLAN: NAVIGATING REAL ESTATE CROWDFUNDING AND SHORT-TERM RENTAL ARBITRAGE

Embarking on a journey to combine Real Estate Crowdfunding and Short-Term Rental Arbitrage requires a systematic and strategic approach. This 30-day action plan provides a step-by-step guide to help investors navigate these two dynamic real estate investment strategies, offering a comprehensive roadmap for success.

Week 1: Research and Education

Day 1-3: Understand Real Estate Crowdfunding Regulations

Begin by familiarizing yourself with the regulatory landscape of Real Estate Crowdfunding. Different regions may have varying regulations, and understanding the legal framework is crucial.

Explore reputable sources, consult legal experts if necessary, and grasp the compliance requirements for crowdfunding investments in your target market.

Day 4-7: Explore Short-Term Rental Market Trends

Delve into the short-term rental market. Understand the demand dynamics, popular destinations, and seasonal trends. Analyze successful arbitrage models and identify key factors that contribute to profitability in short-term rentals. Utilize online resources, industry reports, and case studies to gain insights into the market landscape.

Week 2: Platform Selection and Account Setup

Day 8-10: Identify Suitable Crowdfunding Platforms

Research Real Estate Crowdfunding platforms to find those aligning with your investment goals. Consider factors such as platform reputation, project variety, and fee structures. Read reviews and testimonials from other investors to gauge the platform's reliability and effectiveness. Narrow down your choices to platforms that resonate with your investment strategy.

Day 11-14: Set Up Accounts on Chosen Platforms

Once you've selected your preferred crowdfunding platforms, create accounts and complete the necessary registration processes.

Take the time to explore the platform interfaces, understand their investment offerings, and familiarize yourself with the tools they provide for monitoring and managing your investments.

Week 3: Property Analysis and Due Diligence
Day 15-17: Analyze Potential Crowdfunding Projects

Start evaluating potential crowdfunding projects. Scrutinize project details, financial projections, and the track record of the development teams. Assess the risk and return profiles of different projects to diversify your crowdfunding portfolio effectively. Leverage the analytical tools provided by the platforms to make informed investment decisions.

Day 18-21: Evaluate Properties for Short-Term Rental Arbitrage

Simultaneously, identify potential properties for Short-Term Rental Arbitrage. Conduct market research to pinpoint locations with high rental demand and potential profitability. Begin negotiations with property owners or landlords, considering factors such as lease terms, property condition, and proximity to key amenities or attractions.

Week 4: Strategy Integration and Launch

Day 22-24: Develop a Comprehensive Investment Strategy

Synthesize the information gathered over the past three weeks to create a comprehensive investment strategy. Determine the allocation of funds between crowdfunding and arbitrage, considering your financial goals, risk tolerance, and investment horizon. Establish a timeline for executing your strategy and set measurable objectives.

Day 25-28: Begin Investing in Crowdfunding Projects

Initiate your investment journey by committing funds to selected crowdfunding projects. Monitor the progress of your investments regularly and stay informed about any updates or changes. Utilize the analytical tools provided by the crowdfunding platforms to track the performance of your portfolio and make adjustments if necessary.

Day 29-30: Implement Short-Term Rental Arbitrage Plan

As your crowdfunding investments take shape, shift your focus to implementing the Short-Term Rental Arbitrage plan. Finalize lease agreements, set up your properties for short-term rentals, and launch your listings on relevant platforms.

Implement dynamic pricing strategies to optimize occupancy and maximize rental income. Monitor guest feedback and adjust your approach based on market responses.

Ongoing: Continuous Monitoring and Adjustment

Beyond the initial 30 days, maintain a proactive approach to managing your combined investment portfolio. Continuously monitor the performance of both crowdfunding projects and short-term rentals. Stay informed about market trends, regulatory changes, and emerging opportunities. Adjust your strategies as needed to align with evolving market conditions and ensure the ongoing success of your real estate investment plan.

By following this 30-day action plan, investors can seamlessly integrate Real Estate Crowdfunding and Short-Term Rental Arbitrage into a cohesive and dynamic investment strategy.

This structured approach provides a solid foundation for navigating the complexities of both models, ultimately maximizing the potential for long-term growth and immediate income generation in the realm of real estate investment.

Reader Engagement Section: Implement Your Plan

As you embark on the 30-day action plan, it's time to put your knowledge into action. Consider the following:

I. Share your progress in implementing the plan. What challenges have you encountered, and how have you overcome them?

II. Reflect on any adjustments you've made to your initial strategy. How have market conditions or unexpected factors influenced your decisions?

III. Engaging in these discussions will not only solidify your understanding but also provide a supportive community for ongoing learning.

CASE STUDIES: LEARNING FROM SUCCESSFUL IMPLEMENTATIONS

Exploring real-world case studies is a powerful way to gain insights into the practical application of combined Real Estate Crowdfunding and Short-Term Rental Arbitrage strategies. These examples illustrate how investors have navigated challenges, capitalized on opportunities, and achieved success by seamlessly integrating these two dynamic approaches into their real estate portfolios.

Successful Real Estate Crowdfunding Projects

Case Study 1: Diversifying Across Crowdfunding Platforms

Maria, an investor with a keen interest in residential real estate, decided to diversify her portfolio across multiple crowdfunding platforms. Over a period of two years, she strategically allocated funds to projects ranging from residential developments in urban areas to commercial properties in emerging markets.

By diversifying her investments, Maria mitigated risks associated with individual projects and market fluctuations. The stable growth of her crowdfunding portfolio provided a solid foundation for her broader real estate investment strategy.

Case Study 2: Strategic Allocation for Balanced Returns

John, a seasoned investor, adopted a strategic approach by allocating a portion of his portfolio to Real Estate Crowdfunding while maintaining a diverse range of other investments. His crowdfunded projects included a mix of residential and commercial properties. John carefully monitored the performance of each project and, when certain milestones were achieved, reinvested the returns into new crowdfunding opportunities. This systematic approach allowed him to balance stable, long-term growth with the potential for immediate returns through other investment avenues.

Examples of Profitable Short-Term Rental Arbitrage Ventures

Case Study 1: Urban Short-Term Rentals

Samantha identified a growing demand for short-term rentals in her city's urban center, particularly among business travelers and tourists. She secured favorable long-term leases for well-located apartments and strategically furnished them for short-term stays. Leveraging dynamic pricing strategies, Samantha optimized occupancy rates and achieved high nightly rates during peak seasons. Her meticulous property management and focus on guest satisfaction resulted in positive reviews, encouraging repeat bookings and establishing a steady income stream.

Case Study 2: Seasonal Vacation Rentals

Jake capitalized on the popularity of vacation destinations by targeting properties in seasonal markets. He secured properties near beaches and recreational areas and implemented a seasonal rental strategy.

During peak vacation months, Jake charged premium rates for his short-term rentals, and during off-peak seasons, he adjusted pricing to attract longer-term tenants. This approach allowed him to maximize income during high-demand periods while maintaining occupancy throughout the year.

Integrating Crowdfunding and Arbitrage:
Case Study: Maximizing Returns through Synergy

Emily, an ambitious investor, strategically integrated Real Estate Crowdfunding and Short-Term Rental Arbitrage into her investment plan. She began by allocating a portion of her funds to crowdfunding projects with promising growth potential. As her crowdfunding portfolio matured, Emily redirected returns into short-term rental properties, carefully selecting locations with high rental demand.

Emily's approach involved using the stable returns from crowdfunding to offset the initial costs of arbitrage ventures. The ongoing income generated from short-term rentals provided immediate returns, contributing to the overall financial health of her investment portfolio.

By continually reinvesting returns into new opportunities within both crowdfunding and arbitrage, Emily created a dynamic cycle of growth and income generation.

These case studies showcase the versatility and adaptability of a combined Real Estate Crowdfunding and Short-Term Rental Arbitrage strategy. Investors can draw inspiration from these examples and tailor their approaches based on their unique goals, risk tolerance, and market conditions. Understanding how others have successfully navigated these strategies provides valuable insights for crafting a personalized and effective real estate investment plan.

Key Takeaways from Case Studies:

Diversification is Key: Successful investors strategically diversify their real estate portfolios, both within crowdfunding platforms and across different types of short-term rental properties.

Strategic Allocation and Reinvestment: Investors strategically allocate funds, monitor project performance, and reinvest returns to optimize their overall real estate investment strategy.

Market Awareness and Adaptability: Case studies highlight the importance of staying informed about market trends, regulatory changes, and emerging opportunities. Successful investors adapt their strategies based on evolving market conditions.

Synergy for Maximum Impact: Integrating Real Estate Crowdfunding and Short-Term Rental Arbitrage allows for a dynamic and synergistic approach, maximizing the benefits of stable long-term growth and immediate income generation.

As investors consider implementing a combined strategy, these case studies serve as valuable references, offering practical insights and strategies that can be tailored to individual preferences and goals. The journey to success in real estate investment is dynamic, and learning from the experiences of others can provide a roadmap for navigating the complexities of the market effectively.

Reader Engagement Section: Apply Insights

As you delve into real-world case studies, it's time to apply the insights gained to your own investment approach. Consider the following:

I. Identify key takeaways from each case study. How can you adapt successful strategies to your unique situation?

II. Share your thoughts on how challenges faced by investors in the case studies could be mitigated. What alternative approaches might have been considered?

III. Reflect on how the case studies have influenced your overall perspective on combining Crowdfunding and Arbitrage.

TIPS FOR SUCCESS: FINE-TUNING YOUR REAL ESTATE INVESTMENT APPROACH

Embarking on a journey to combine Real Estate Crowdfunding and Short-Term Rental Arbitrage requires not only a comprehensive understanding of the strategies but also a set of practical tips to fine-tune your approach. These tips are distilled from the experiences of successful investors who have navigated the intricacies of both models, providing valuable insights for those seeking to optimize their real estate portfolios.

Building a Robust Real Estate Portfolio:

Tip 1: Diversify Across Property Types and Locations

Diversification is a fundamental principle in building a resilient real estate portfolio. In the realm of Real Estate Crowdfunding, consider diversifying across different property types (residential, commercial, development projects) and geographic locations.

This diversity helps mitigate risks associated with specific markets or property sectors.

Tip 2: Leverage Real Estate Crowdfunding for Long-Term Stability

Real Estate Crowdfunding offers stability and the potential for long-term growth. Allocate a portion of your funds to crowdfunding projects that align with your investment goals. These projects can serve as the bedrock of your portfolio, providing a steady income stream and potential appreciation over time.

Tip 3: Stay Informed About Market Trends

Successful investors in Real Estate Crowdfunding are proactive in staying informed about market trends. Regularly monitor updates from crowdfunding platforms, analyze market reports, and stay attuned to economic indicators. This awareness allows you to adapt your portfolio strategy based on evolving market conditions.

Navigating Challenges in Crowdfunding and Arbitrage:

Tip 4: Conduct Thorough Due Diligence in Crowdfunding

Due diligence is paramount when selecting crowdfunding projects. Scrutinize project details, financial projections, and the track record of development teams. Engage with the community on crowdfunding platforms, participate in forums, and seek insights from experienced investors. Thorough due diligence is a crucial step in minimizing risks and maximizing returns.

Tip 5: Establish a Robust Arbitrage Operational Framework

Short-Term Rental Arbitrage demands a hands-on operational approach. Establish a robust framework for property management, guest communication, and maintenance. Implement efficient systems for check-ins, cleanings, and routine inspections. A well-organized operational structure is essential for success in the dynamic world of short-term rentals.

Tip 6: Adapt to Market Conditions

Both Crowdfunding and Arbitrage are influenced by market conditions. Be agile in adapting your strategies based on changing economic landscapes, local market dynamics, and regulatory shifts. This adaptability ensures that your real estate investments remain resilient in the face of challenges and capitalize on emerging opportunities.

Staying Informed about Market Trends:

Tip 7: Continuously Monitor Crowdfunding Investments

Regularly monitor the performance of your crowdfunding investments. Leverage the analytical tools provided by crowdfunding platforms to track the progress of projects, assess returns, and identify any red flags. Continuous monitoring allows you to make informed decisions, whether it's reinvesting returns or adjusting your portfolio allocation.

Tip 8: Utilize Technology for Short-Term Rental Success

In Short-Term Rental Arbitrage, technology can be a powerful ally. Utilize property management systems, dynamic pricing tools, and automation to streamline operations. Embrace digital marketing strategies to enhance the visibility of your rentals on online platforms. Technology not only improves efficiency but also enhances the overall guest experience.

Tip 9: Prioritize Guest Satisfaction in Short-Term Rentals

Positive guest experiences are paramount in the world of short-term rentals. Prioritize cleanliness, thoughtful amenities, and responsive communication. Implement guest feedback mechanisms and use reviews as valuable insights for improvement. Satisfied guests are more likely to return and recommend your property to others.

Strategic Planning for Long-Term Success:

Tip 10: Reinvest Crowdfunding Returns Strategically

As returns accumulate from your crowdfunding investments, devise a strategic plan for reinvestment. Assess the performance of your portfolio, identify new opportunities, and allocate returns in a way that aligns with your overall investment goals. Strategic reinvestment enhances the potential for continued growth.

Tip 11: Plan for Economic Cycles

Real estate markets are subject to economic cycles. Plan your investment strategy with an awareness of these cycles. During economic downturns, opportunities for distressed properties may arise, while economic upswings may present ideal conditions for short-term rental profitability. Understanding and planning for economic cycles positions you to capitalize on market fluctuations.

Tip 12: Seek Professional Advice When Needed

Consider seeking advice from financial advisors, real estate professionals, or legal experts, especially when dealing with significant investment decisions or navigating complex regulatory landscapes. Professional guidance can provide valuable insights and help you make well-informed decisions aligned with your financial objectives.

Implementing these tips requires a blend of strategic planning, market awareness, and operational excellence. Whether you are a seasoned investor or just starting, these insights can guide you in building a robust and dynamic real estate investment approach that encompasses both Real Estate Crowdfunding and Short-Term Rental Arbitrage. As you fine-tune your strategies and navigate the evolving real estate landscape, these tips serve as valuable tools for success in the realm of combined real estate investment.

Reader Engagement Section: Refine Your Strategy

As you explore tips for success, it's time to refine and enhance your real estate investment approach. Reflect on the following:

I. Which tips resonate most with your investment philosophy? How can you incorporate these into your strategy?

II.   Share your own tips or insights that align with the principles discussed in this chapter. How have you successfully fine-tuned your approach?

III. Discuss any challenges you foresee in implementing these tips and seek advice from the online community.

RISK MANAGEMENT STRATEGIES: SAFEGUARDING YOUR REAL ESTATE INVESTMENT PORTFOLIO

Navigating the dynamic landscape of Real Estate Crowdfunding and Short-Term Rental Arbitrage requires a robust risk management strategy. While these investment approaches offer lucrative opportunities, they are not without challenges. Implementing effective risk management strategies is essential for safeguarding your real estate investment portfolio and ensuring long-term success.

Understanding and Assessing Risks:

Tip 1: Conduct Comprehensive Due Diligence

Thorough due diligence is the foundation of effective risk management. Before committing funds to crowdfunding projects or engaging in Short-Term Rental Arbitrage, conduct extensive research. Evaluate project details, financial projections, and the backgrounds of project developers.

For arbitrage, scrutinize the local rental market, property conditions, and regulatory landscapes. Identifying potential risks early on allows you to make informed decisions and mitigate potential challenges.

Tip 2: Diversify Your Investments

Diversification is a powerful risk mitigation strategy. Spread your investments across various crowdfunding projects, property types, and geographic locations. Diversifying your real estate portfolio minimizes the impact of a poor-performing project or a downturn in a specific market. A well-diversified portfolio is more resilient to market fluctuations and economic uncertainties.

Tip 3: Stay Informed about Market Trends and Economic Indicators

Actively monitor market trends and economic indicators that may impact real estate. Stay informed about interest rates, employment figures, and housing market trends. Recognizing potential shifts in the economic landscape allows you to adjust your investment strategy proactively.

Be particularly attuned to factors that may affect short-term rental demand, such as local events, tourism trends, and regulatory changes.

Risk Mitigation in Crowdfunding:

Tip 4: Choose Platforms with a Proven Track Record

Selecting reputable crowdfunding platforms is crucial for mitigating risks in Real Estate Crowdfunding. Opt for platforms with a proven track record, transparent communication, and a history of successful project completions. Research platform reviews, user experiences, and the platform's overall reputation within the real estate investment community.

Tip 5: Assess Project-Specific Risks

Each crowdfunding project carries its own set of risks. Evaluate project-specific risks, such as construction delays, market fluctuations, or changes in local regulations. Consider the track record of the development team and their ability to navigate potential challenges.

Understanding project-specific risks allows you to make informed investment decisions aligned with your risk tolerance.

Tip 6: Monitor and Adjust Portfolio Allocation

Regularly assess the performance of your crowdfunding portfolio and adjust your allocation based on project progress and market conditions. If certain projects face challenges or if market dynamics shift, consider reallocating funds to projects with more favorable risk-return profiles. A dynamic and adaptive portfolio allocation strategy enhances your ability to manage risks effectively.

Risk Mitigation in Short-Term Rental Arbitrage:

Tip 7: Comply with Local Regulations

Regulatory compliance is a critical aspect of risk mitigation in Short-Term Rental Arbitrage. Familiarize yourself with local regulations governing short-term rentals, zoning laws, and licensing requirements. Regulation violations may result in cash penalties as well as legal problems.

Stay updated on any changes in local legislation that may impact your short-term rental operations.

Tip 8: Implement Robust Operational Practices

Operational efficiency is key to mitigating risks in short-term rentals. Establish robust property management practices, including regular maintenance, thorough cleanings between guests, and efficient communication with guests. Implementing effective operational practices reduces the likelihood of negative guest experiences, property damage, or regulatory violations.

Tip 9: Stay Responsive to Market Conditions

Short-term rental success is closely tied to market conditions. Stay responsive to changes in demand, seasonal variations, and economic shifts. Adjust pricing strategies, marketing efforts, and property amenities based on market dynamics. Being attuned to market conditions enhances your ability to optimize occupancy and rental income while minimizing risks associated with fluctuating demand.

Mitigating Overall Portfolio Risks:

Tip 10: Establish an Emergency Fund

Unforeseen circumstances can impact both crowdfunding projects and short-term rentals. Establishing an emergency fund provides a financial cushion to address unexpected expenses, project delays, or periods of low rental occupancy. An emergency fund adds a layer of security to your overall real estate investment portfolio.

Tip 11: Regularly Reassess Your Risk Tolerance

As market conditions evolve, reassess your risk tolerance periodically. Your risk tolerance may change based on personal circumstances, economic outlook, or changes in investment goals. Adjust your investment strategy to align with your current risk tolerance, ensuring that your real estate portfolio remains well-suited to your financial objectives.

Tip 12: Seek Professional Advice for Complex Matters

For complex matters such as legal issues, tax implications, or major investment decisions, consider seeking professional advice. Consult with legal professionals, tax advisors, or financial planners to ensure that your real estate investment strategy aligns with legal requirements and optimizes your financial position.

By implementing these risk management strategies, investors can fortify their real estate portfolios against potential challenges. Real Estate Crowdfunding and Short-Term Rental Arbitrage offer diverse opportunities, and effective risk management is key to maximizing returns while minimizing potential downsides. As you fine-tune your risk management approach, remember that a well-informed and adaptive strategy is the cornerstone of long-term success in the dynamic world of real estate investment.

Reader Engagement Section: Develop Your Risk Mitigation Plan

As you delve into risk management strategies, it's time to develop a personalized plan to safeguard your investment portfolio. Consider the following:

I.   Identify specific risks associated with your real estate investments. How can you mitigate these risks based on the strategies discussed in this chapter?

II. Share your risk mitigation plan with fellow readers. How have you tailored it to your unique investment goals and risk tolerance?

III. Discuss any additional risks not covered in the chapter and seek insights from the community on effective risk management.

IV. Engaging in these discussions will empower you to develop a robust risk mitigation plan that aligns with your overall investment strategy.